Charles Drew

Published in the United States of America by Cherry Lake Publishing
Ann Arbor, Michigan
www.cherrylakepublishing.com

Content Adviser: Jessica Criales, Doctoral Candidate, History Department, Rutgers University
Reading Adviser: Marla Conn MS, Ed., Literacy specialist, Read-Ability, Inc.
Book Design: Jennifer Wahi
Illustrator: Jeff Bane

Photo Credits: ©Victor Maschek/Shutterstock, 5; ©Steve Rosset/Shutterstock, 7; ©lenetstan/Shutterstock, 9; ©fri9thsep/Shutterstock, 11, 22; ©imging/Shutterstock, 13, 23; ©PD-USGov, 15; ©Happy cake Happy cafe/Shutterstock, 17; ©PD-USGov-HHS Harris and Ewing, 19; ©PD-USGov, 21, Cover, 8, 10, 12, Jeff Bane; Various frames throughout, ©Shutterstock Images

Library of Congress Cataloging-in-Publication Data

Names: Marsico, Katie, 1980- author.
Title: Charles Drew / by Katie Marsico.
Description: Ann Arbor : Cherry Lake Publishing, 2018. | Series: My
  itty-bitty bio | Audience: K to grade 3. | Includes bibliographical
  references and index.
Identifiers: LCCN 2018003106| ISBN 9781534128798 (hardcover) | ISBN
  9781534130494 (pdf) | ISBN 9781534131996 (paperback) | ISBN 9781534133693
  (hosted ebook)
Subjects: LCSH: Drew, Charles, 1904-1950--Juvenile literature. |
  Surgeons--United States--Biography--Juvenile literature. | African
  American surgeons--United States--Biography--Juvenile literature. |
  Blood--Collection and preservation--History--Juvenile literature.
Classification: LCC RD27.35.D74 M37 2018 | DDC 617.092 [B] --dc23
LC record available at https://lccn.loc.gov/2018003106

Printed in the United States of America
Corporate Graphics

table of contents

About the author: Katie Marsico is the author of more than 200 reference books for children and young adults. She lives with her husband and six children near Chicago, Illinois.

About the illustrator: Jeff Bane and his two business partners own a studio along the American River in Folsom, California, home of the 1849 Gold Rush. When Jeff's not sketching or illustrating for clients, he's either swimming or kayaking in the river to relax.

I was born in Washington, DC.

Back then, blacks didn't have the same rights as whites.

I was lucky. I went to good schools.

Later, I got into college.

When do you feel lucky?

I wanted to become a doctor.

Some schools didn't take black students.

I studied medicine in Canada. I learned how to do a **transfusion**.

This gives one person's blood to someone else.

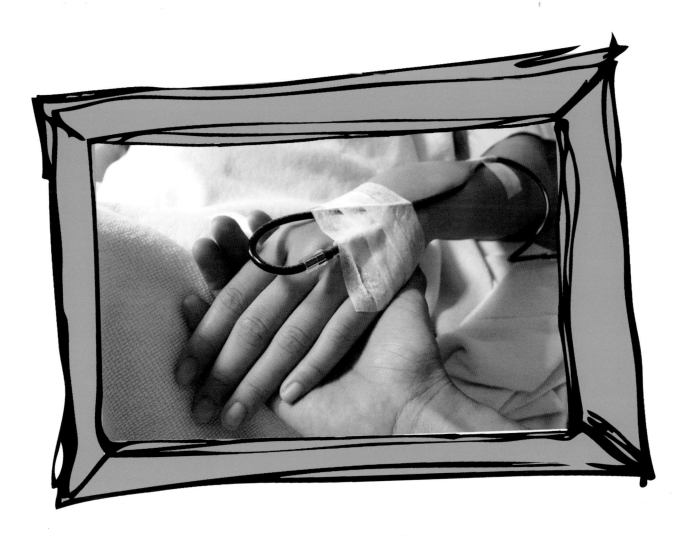

I returned to work in the United States.

I set up a **blood bank** for transfusions.

Soon more blood banks formed. They were important during wars.

People who were hurt needed blood.

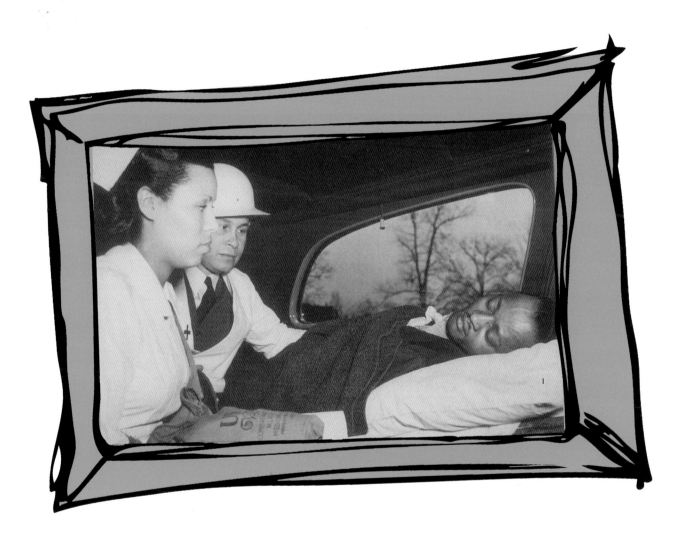

Healthy people gave blood.
Yet I couldn't at first.

Blacks were told they couldn't give blood.

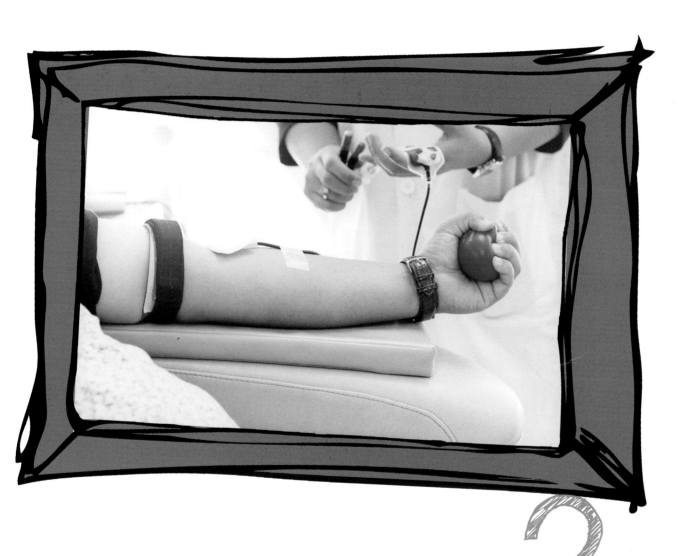

What do you think about this rule?

I spoke out for **equality**.

I said medical schools should treat blacks fairly.

Why is fairness important?

I was in a car **accident**. I died in 1950. But my work with blood banks saved lives.

I taught others about equal rights. I showed that **segregation** and science don't mix!

What would you like to ask me?

1933

1900

Born
1904

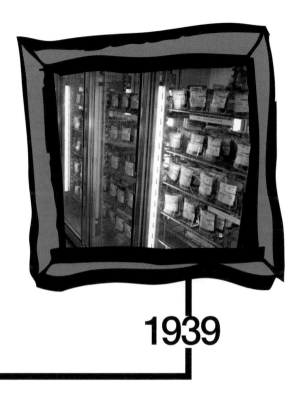

1939

2000

Died
1950

glossary

accident (AK-sih-duhnt) an unlucky and unplanned event

blood bank (BLUHD BANGK) a place where people go to give blood and then that blood is stored for use later

equality (ih-KWAH-lih-tee) the right of everyone to be treated the same

segregation (seh-grih-GAY-shuhn) the act of treating a group of people differently or unfairly, often because of their race or religion

transfusion (tranz-FYOO-zhuhn) the act of moving blood from one person to another person who needs it

index